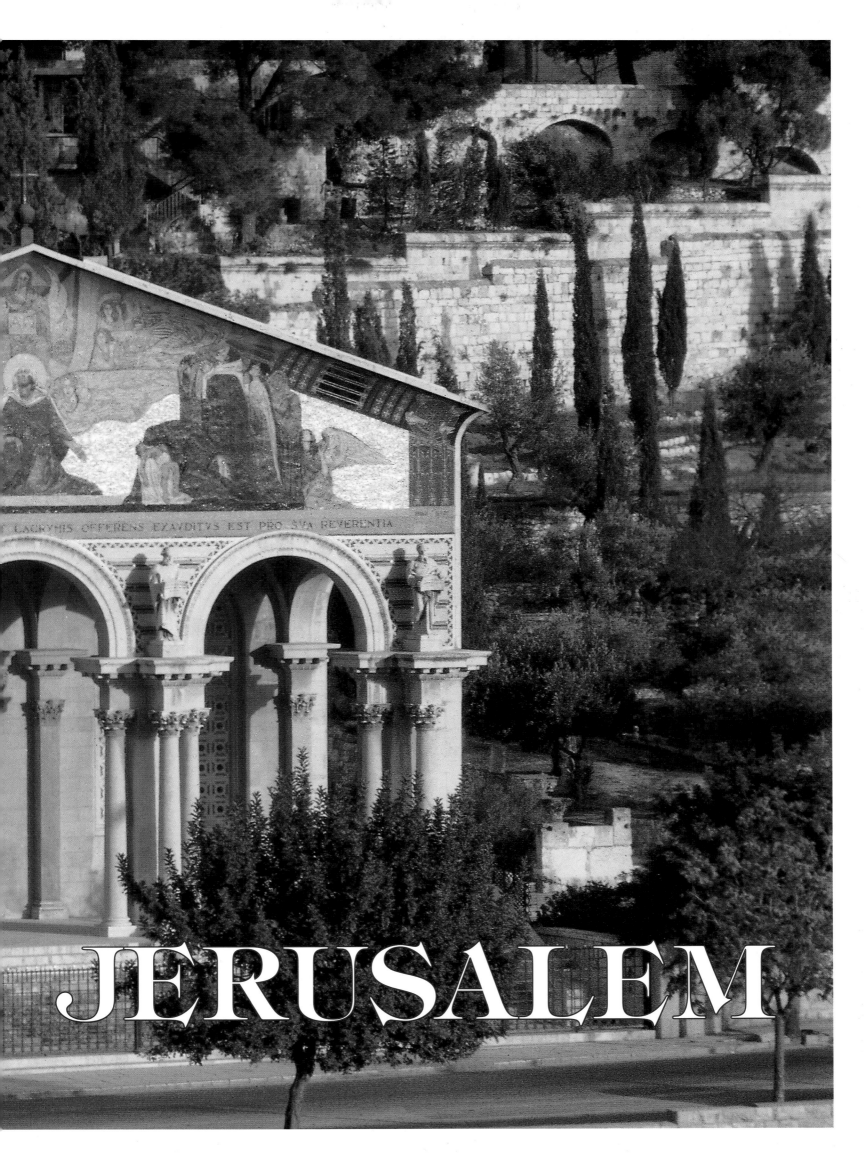

LACRYMIS OFFERENS EXAVDITVS EST PRO SVA REVERENTIA

JERUSALEM

1

A city in triplicate

Jerusalem is unique. There is no other word for it. The city nestles between mountains, fertile plains and the Judea Desert: it is easy to see how Jerusalem was thought by people in Biblical times to be at the centre of the earth. This sense of importance is highlighted by the rich history of the city – sacred to followers of Judaism, Christianity and Islam – and its ethnic diversity of culture, language and mood.

Set at the climatic junction of Asia, Africa and Europe, Jerusalem has blistering hot summers and severe winters. But it is truly a city for all seasons – its individual charm lying in its historical testimony even more than in the physical beauty of its buildings. Periodic upheaval caused by revolution and war in the Old City ever since King David's rule has proved that stories last longer than stone. The twentieth century continued this long process of change in Jerusalem. The state of Israel was formed, encouraging displaced Jews to make their way to Jerusalem; political control of the city changed hands at least three times; and Jerusalem's ancient walls were breached physically and psychologically to form new centres and suburbs to cope with refugees from anti-Semitic regimes and the survivors of the Holocaust.

Modern Jerusalem is made up of three sections. The Old City is what most people regard as "Jerusalem", the Biblical settlement which has survived to this day. West Jerusalem, the New City, spreads westwards beyond the Jaffa Gate in the city wall. This was the only direction in which to expand free of natural barriers. West Jerusalem is the state capital and administrative centre of Israel. East Jerusalem is a Palestinian community of homes, businesses, hotels – and a separate university – perched between the north wall of the Old City and the mountains

RUSTIC
URNITURE
and
TILES

ריהוט כפר
ואריחים

7

7: *Street trader*

8: *Street scene*

9: *Souvenirs of coloured sand*

8

11

10: *Market porter*

11: *Street scene*

12: *Selling bananas at a market*

beyond. It is said that the Old City is best visited by day and the New City by night, to see famous sites in their best light and to return to the suburbs to enjoy Jerusalem's modern leisure facilities.

Jerusalem does not have a homogeneous culture: the 600,000 people who live in the city provide a patchwork mix of races and creeds which enrich the community. The balance of political power is currently held by secular and modern orthodox Jews. Yet one third of the population is not Jewish at all: most of this group are Muslims – but the 30,000 Christians who live in the city comprise an influential minority. Such cultural differences between Jerusalem's many religious groups are highlighted by local dietary traditions. For all

12

13

that, the normal everyday menu in the city nearly always includes a range of beans and spices. Chicken is the meat eaten most frequently. So there may be profound contrasts between the peoples of Jerusalem, and individuals may have deeply held views, but humour, family values, pragmatism and an enduring sense of humanity usually win through any cultural misunderstandings. Jerusalem is a city of kaleidoscopic qualities. Its history and culture gently challenge the visitor to think about life's important questions.

Jerusalem is not a city equipped for fleeting tourists, although cafes and restaurants are becoming increasingly prominent in both West and East Jerusalem. The main leisure pursuit of its people is reading, a lifestyle developed through religious practice and academic endeavour. Secular books, particularly those written in Hebrew, are also popular. Music in the city tends to be either classical, religious or traditional; there are several international festivals held in Jerusalem that celebrate each genre. Art as a medium is less pronounced, given the religious practice of orthodox Jews and Muslims not to depict "graven images", but the visual sense is more than fulfilled by the antiquity of the place – archaeology is a pastime pursued with vigour by enthusiastic locals.

Many people arrive for the first time with strong personal concepts of what Jerusalem will be like. Nonetheless, for pilgrims and tourists who show curiosity and a lack of prejudice the reality of Jerusalem will surprise and excite. Their most unexpected realisation may be that after several millennia of turmoil Jerusalem is starting to live up to one of its Hebrew meanings, the "City of Peace".

15

A turbulent but occasionally glorious past

Jerusalem has always had religious significance: even its name once meant "the city of [the god] Shalem", referring to one of the ancient deities of pre-Israelite days. A city-state existed on the site of Jerusalem during the Bronze Age in around 2500 BCE, but the region's first significant event took place some 500 years later, when the patriarch Abraham dutifully prepared himself to sacrifice his son Isaac on Mount Moriah, close to the original city. Jerusalem then remained a backwater for nigh on ten centuries because its location gave no natural or military advantage to prospective invaders.

King David was the first leader to unite the traditional Twelve Tribes of Israel. He seized Jerusalem for his capital from the incumbent Jebusites in 1000 BCE because the area held no symbolic meaning for any of the Tribes and was therefore acceptable to all. Only later was the link with Abraham realised and the religious importance of Jerusalem to the Jewish people established.

King David brought the Ark of the Covenant containing the Ten Commandments to Jerusalem, but the task of building a Temple to house them fell to his son and heir, Solomon, in about 950 BCE. When King Solomon died in 922 BCE, however, rival tensions among the Jewish tribes resurfaced which led – 17 years later – to a split in the kingdom. Ten dissident tribes formed a new kingdom of Israel, in Samaria to the north,

and the remaining two loyal to David's dynasty became Judah, and kept Jerusalem as their kingdom's capital. Civil war followed, which weakened all the tribes and lay the region open to attack. Israel fell to the Assyrians in 721 BCE, and all its people were sent into exile. Judah held out, thanks to the military foresight of King Hezekiah in securing a reliable water supply for Jerusalem, and to the religious fervour inspired in the people there by the prophet Isaiah.

But in time Judah eventually found itself caught between two powerful states – the Egyptians and the Babylonians. King Zedekiah of Judah backed the wrong side, and the Babylonians invaded in 587 BCE. Their king, Nebuchadnezzar, destroyed Solomon's Temple in Jerusalem in revenge, and forced the remaining Jews into exile in Babylon itself. The Babylonians were, however, defeated in turn in 539 BCE by the Persians, whose benevolent dictator King Cyrus allowed those Jews who wanted to return to Jerusalem. He even donated money for the rebuilding of the Temple, which was completed in 515 BCE. The city walls were improved by Nehemiah, a Jewish official from Persia.

18

19

18: The Tomb of David

19: Nebuchadnezzar's siege of Jerusalem

20: 'Massacre of the Innocents by Herod's soldiers'
Matteo di Giovanni (ca 1435–1495), 1482, Church of St. Agostino, Siena

Even this defence could not prevent Jerusalem from being taken by the forces of Alexander the Great in 331 BCE. Greek rule was first supervised by the Hellenic Ptolemies in Egypt and then by the Seleucids from Syria. Resistance to Greek religious dogma sparked a successful Jewish revolution in 167 BCE, led by Judah the Maccabee (Judas Maccabaeus). The ensuing Hasmonean dynasty of princelings was riven with family squabbles, enabling the Romans under Pompey to take control of the region in 63 BCE. Herod the Great was soon installed as ruler, for he had been born in the region and yet retained excellent contacts in Rome. A vain and paranoid tyrant, Herod nevertheless built important structures such as the palace that was also the regional military headquarters (the "fortress") and enlarged the Temple, thereafter widely regarded as an architectural wonder.

21: Effigy of the sleeping Virgin Mary inside Dormition Abbey

22: Aerial view of the Temple Esplanade from the south-west

21

Herod was finally deposed in a bloody coup in 4 BCE. At around this time, Jesus was born in Bethlehem, a town close to Jerusalem: it was an event that in due course would change the world. Contemporary evidence shows that Jesus was critical of materialism and religious hypocrisy. He promoted the practice of neighbourly love, but was eventually arrested in 33 CE following his very public criticism of the Romans and their system of governance by procurator. Pontius Pilate, the fifth incumbent, sentenced Jesus to death by crucifixion – a commonplace punishment. News of Jesus' life and work was slow to spread: the new religion was given most impetus by Paul (formerly Saul) of Tarsus (later to be acclaimed by Christians as an apostle and saint).

In 66 CE Jerusalem revolted against Rome after Emperor Caligula tried to redesign the Temple in his own image. A bloody war ensued which the Roman general Titus won four years later, destroying the Temple and forcing the Jewish nation to scatter in all directions (the "diaspora" or dispersal). Continuing resistance caused Emperor Hadrian to raze Jerusalem to the ground and build a new city, Aelia Capitolina, in which only the established Roman deities were permitted. The street pattern laid down marked out the "quarters" which exist to this day: remains of such roads as Cardo and Decumanus have been discovered.

23

The Byzantine Emperor Constantine's conversion to Christianity led him in 325 CE to despatch his mother Helena to Jerusalem to rediscover the "holy places" of the religion. She deduced that Hadrian would have erected his temples on the holiest sites, and soon discovered remnants of the "True Cross" at a temple dedicated to Venus. Constantine commissioned the building of the Church of the Holy Sepulchre on the spot – the site of Jesus' execution. Judaism was seen as a potential threat to Christianity, so its followers were banished.

24

In 638 CE Byzantine rule came to an end when the Muslim Caliph Omar ibn Khattab took over Jerusalem, assisted by Jewish armies. The Caliph brought the Prophet Muhammad's new religion of Islam to the city, which is even today regarded as the third most important centre of the Muslim world. The site of the former temple was chosen as sacred land for an important mosque – for not only was Abraham an important patriarch of Islam but the rock was also the place from which Muhammad was taken up into heaven. The Dome of the Rock mosque was completed in 691. The initial religious tolerance gave way to persecution of Christians and, by the eleventh century, desecration of holy sites. Matters got so bad that Pope Urban II actively recruited religious-minded European knights to reclaim the holy land for Christianity, and

23: *The Cardo in the Jewish Quarter*

24: *The Old City walls at night*

25: *Aerial view of the Ophel Archaeological Gardens*

in 1099 the Crusaders accordingly took Jerusalem – but wiped out the city's population of 40,000 inhabitants. Despite enhanced defences, the city was won back for Islam in 1187. Further Crusades failed to oust various Muslim regimes over several centuries.

In 1517 Jerusalem became part of the Ottoman Empire. Suleyman (Suleiman) the Magnificent came to power almost immediately afterwards and began a massive building programme of mosques, water-supply channels and city walls. Many of these structures survive to this day. Jerusalem's strategic value declined after Suleyman's reign and the region was dominated by various warlords and Bedouin chiefs until the mid-nineteenth century. In 1831 an Egyptian leader called Mohammed Ali took power and through personal charisma created enough political stability and religious tolerance in the region for foreign interest in Jerusalem to return, often in the guise of "looking after the holy sites".

The crowded city finally burst through the confines of its walls when people found it safer to risk attack from out-laws on the outside than remain vulnerable to epidemic diseases within. Foreign benefactors (such as Sir Moses Montefiore from Britain) donated funds to build new suburbs to the west of the Old City. Political upheaval then prevalent in many countries caused Jews to emigrate from them to Jerusalem, so these suburbs expanded quickly to meet the demand. The process was fuelled further by militant Zionism, the movement to re-establish the state of Israel as a national homeland for Jews.

British troops captured Jerusalem from the Ottoman Turks in 1917. In 1922 the city became the centre of the League of Nations mandate by which Britain governed the territory with a view to establishing a nation-state for both Jews and Palestinian Arabs under the terms of the Balfour Declaration. The idea was for the area and the city to be ruled fairly by all sides, but in practice the British became caught in the middle of old religious tensions. Eventually, in the aftermath of World War II, global revulsion over the Nazi Holocaust and some vicious anti-British terrorist activity in the region itself, Israel gained independence in 1948.

The new nation was soon at war with its all-Arab neighbours. Jerusalem had been divided between communities and so became a key focus of the conflict. The brief but ferocious Six-Day War in 1967 unified the city under Israeli control, but hearts and minds were slower to mend. Tensions have tended to remain high in the region, yet the religious importance of Jerusalem to all the monotheist creeds is a symbolic reminder of the potential for people to live in harmony together. And the Hebrew word *shalom* is now regarded as a universal greeting of peace.

26

26–28: *A selection of Holocaust memorials at Yad Vashem*

27

The Citadel

The Citadel sits at the western city wall by the Jaffa Gate, overlooking the evolving sprawl of West Jerusalem. It consists of five majestic towers that reinforce the wall most vulnerable to attack in former times and that in part represent a remnant of King Herod's fortress-palace of 2,000 years ago, which the paranoid tyrant built because as a Roman collaborator he was afraid of being attacked by fellow-Jews in the city. Despite the popular misconception, the Citadel is in no way linked historically with King David.

Its crenellated stone ruins serve as a microcosm of history for the whole city – and the views are breathtaking.

From the second century BCE the site of the Citadel had been an important focal point of authority for Jewish leaders; it was the highest point in the region and so symbolised royal power over the people. Herod reinforced the site with three enormous towers inspired by the ancient lighthouse in Alexandria. These were subsequently demolished by the Roman Emperor Hadrian in 135 CE when he built his new city, Aelia Capitolina. But during the Crusades a millennium later the Citadel was restored, again for defence – boiling liquids were poured through embrasures in the rebuilt towers on to advancing soldiers – and then further embellished under Turkish rule, including the distinctive stone minaret.

Since 1967 the Citadel's museum has been an appropriate starting-point for any visit to Jerusalem because the site reflects the rich history of all three monotheist religions in the city. The museum features artefacts used through the ages and a model of Jerusalem in 1860. In summer, its frequent *son-et-lumière* ("sound and light") shows provide the visitor with a romantic flavour of the Old City. A place like the Citadel makes it easy to imagine travelling back thousands of years in time to relive Jerusalem's vibrant past.

Previous page:

29: Archaeological excavations at the Citadel

30: Aerial view of the Citadel

31: Jaffa Gate

Following page:

32: A street of Jerusalem

The Jewish Quarter

The Jewish Quarter occupies the south-eastern corner of the Old City. It reached its height of influence at the time of King Herod, but in the last 2,000 years its appearance has changed many times without losing its character. Jews were forced to abandon this part of Jerusalem when the Roman general Titus imposed the diaspora in 70 CE. It was not until Israel won the Six-Day War in 1967 that Jews reclaimed this historic quarter, so important symbolically to their faith.

The present-day look to the area is one of stark cleanliness. The stonework is washed, the narrow streets are immaculate, and even the ruins look sharply defined yet strangely natural. There is little if any park land or green space. The Jewish Quarter was razed to the ground (again) after the 1948 war, when Jordan seized control of this section of the city. Such destruction merely mirrored previous events in history such as the dismantling of King Solomon's Temple and its Herodian replacement at regular 1,000-year intervals in ancient times.

In rebuilding the quarter after 1967, the Israelis have made some startling archaeological finds of worldwide significance which have achieved fair scientific prominence. Excavations below modern-day street level have revealed extensive sections of Roman roads such as Cardo, parts of which have now been buried beneath exclusive shopping malls. A house that belonged to Temple priests and that was burned down in 70 CE is a direct link to the Roman invasion led by Titus. Six buildings from the Herodian period have now been revealed containing formal bathing-pools and featuring mosaic surfaces. Other more recent buildings, such as the Hurvà Synagogue and the Tireret Israel Synagogue, have been left as ruins to provide poignant reminders of Jewish suffering over many centuries.

They also provide testament to the practical difficulty people have over agreeing on plans for renovation.

The most dynamic symbol of the Jewish faith's ability to overcome adversity is the Western (Wailing) Wall. This fragment of wall once supported the esplanade to Herod's Temple,

35

36

Previous page:

33: Aerial view of the open-air synagogue at the Wailing Wall

34: Gate entrance to the Wailing Wall courtyard

35: Groups of prayers at the Wailing Wall in different and traditional costumes

36: Jewish man reading scripture at the Wailing Wall

38

37: Israelian Girl eating an ice-lolly

38: A Jew in traditional dress

although not part of the Temple complex itself. It remains 15 metres (48 feet) high and, through its continued existence, in the minds of the faithful represents the steadfastness of God in the context of more than 2,000 years of oppression of the Jewish nation. The Wall is one of the holiest sites in the Judaic world. Under the rule of Byzantine Christianity, Jews were allowed to visit the Wall just once a year, on the 9th day of Av. This date in the Jewish calendar remains one of joyous celebration.

Pilgrims engage in near-silent dialogue with the Wall. Prayers written on pieces of paper are crammed by devotees into gaps in the masonry. Jews are not allowed onto the site of the Temple esplanade itself for fear of inadvertently stepping into the "Holy of Holies" area of King Solomon's first Temple. The square in front of the Wall is a vast open-air synagogue, which becomes a mass of worshippers during major Jewish festivals and even during the weekly observance of the Shabbat (Sabbath). Private bar-mitzvah (coming-of-age) ceremonies are commonplace.

39: Silhouette of Ashkenazi Jewish man at dusk

40: Public staircase in the Old City

41: Menorah on display at the Israel Museum

42: Street scene

Jews flock to the Wailing Wall from all over the world. Ultra-orthodox Ashkenazim come from Europe and speak Yiddish, the Hebraic dialect of German. The men wear black frock-coats and hats with fur brims. They often have long beards and dangling sidelocks. Married Ashkenazi women keep their heads covered at all times. Sephardic Jews from Spain and Portugal speak the Ladino dialect. Their rituals differ from those of the Ashkenazim. North African and Middle-Eastern Jews wear embroidered caps, similar to Islamic headgear. The mood at the Wall is often one of personal solemn reflection, a disposition which the Jewish Quarter inspires in everyone who visits the area.

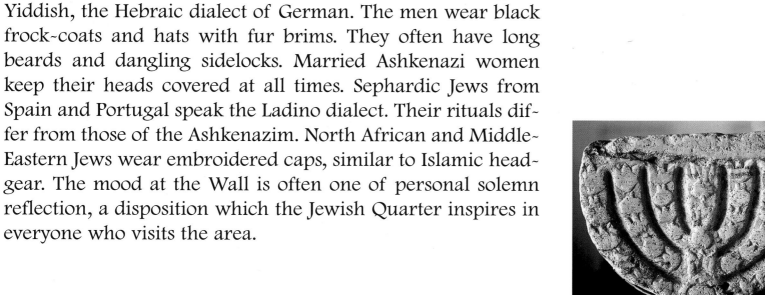

The Christian Quarter

Ever since Jesus was crucified there, Christian influence in Jerusalem has waxed and waned. Byzantine patrons and then Crusading knights built lasting monuments to their faith all over the city. For example, the well-preserved Church of St Anne – by tradition marking the birthplace of the Virgin Mary and the home of her parents – survives unscathed in the Muslim Quarter. It was constructed in 1142 when the Knights Templar were at the zenith of their Crusader power. Although the modern Christian Quarter occupies the north-western portion of the Old City, the true spirit of the neighbourhood shines through only when it is approached through the Muslim Quarter, from the Lion's Gate along the Via Dolorosa.

One of the most important traditions for Catholic and Orthodox Christians concerns the fourteen "stations" along the Via Dolorosa that together make up the formalised "Way of the Cross" which commemorates Jesus' last walk from his prison in the Roman Antonia Fortress to his execution on Calvary. It is specifically remembered every Friday by a ritualised yet emotional procession led by Franciscan monks. Muslims consider Jesus

a great prophet of Islam, so there is no religious friction in celebrating his life and death in this way. Every "station of the Cross" is marked with plaques on religious buildings. The first station of the cross is located in the courtyard of El-Omary Madrassah (the school of Islamic studies), which occupies the site where Jesus was condemned to death. The last five stations of the cross are located in probably the holiest Christian location in the world: the Church of the Holy Sepulchre.

The Holy Sepulchre is sacred to all Christian denominations (except perhaps to jealous nineteenth-century Protestants who made competing claims for the Garden Tomb, now proven to be the remains of fifth-century BCE burial chambers). The church stands on the site of Jesus' crucifixion, death and burial. Evidence for this includes the facts that people are recorded as having prayed at the site before Titus' invasion of 66 CE – which they would not have done other than for a highly unusual and revered personage – and that the huge expense and even greater

45

46

Previous page:

43: The Christian Quarter with the belltower of the Church of the Redeemer in the distance

44: Via Dolorosa

45: Religious ceremony

46: Ornate marble altar

47: Belltower of the Holy Sepulchre Church

pains that the early Christians went to in placing the church on this exact spot could have been avoided by siting the buildings differently by a few metres.

Centuries of inter-faith wrangling between six different Christian denominations and several devastating fires have resulted in a hotch-potch of architectural styles and decor in this holy place. The result is awe-inspiring, even for non-believers, if perhaps a little garish. The oil-lamps, icons, relics and paintings vie for the visitor's attention, making a simple and reverent pilgrimage to the site more problematical than it might otherwise be. Only the lack of space in Jesus' tomb itself finally evokes a humbling sense of what actually happened on Calvary.

On Holy Saturday as Easter Day approaches, candles are lit in the tomb so that "the Light of the World" may be seen to emanate from the grave – a "New Fire" ritual with inherent dangers. By contrast, the Katholicon (comprising the Greek

choirstalls and nave) provides a vast, austere space without any of the decorative trimmings of the chapel and the tomb. Tradition has it that the space beneath the dome of the transept connects the Holy Sepulchre with the centre of the earth, as if joined by some mystical umbilical cord.

The rest of the Christian Quarter – which includes the Muristan area that encompasses the Lutheran Church of the Redeemer – is typified by markets in which vigorous trading tends to impart a decidedly Greek atmosphere and lift the mood of the area out of sombre contemplation of Jesus' last days on earth.

48

49

48: Courtyard and entrance to the Church of the Holy Sepulchre

49: Mosaic of Jesus and his twelve Apostles

50: Crown of thorns motif under a church dome

Previous page:

51: A typical altarpiece inside a church in the Christian Quarter

52: Mosaic of Virgin and Child

53: Church of St. Anne

54: Virgin with Child in the Holy Sepulchre Church

55: Gate entrance of the Holy Sepulchre Church

The Muslim Quarter

The Muslim Quarter of the Old City is bound by the north-eastern portion of the walls. It is the largest and most animated quarter, with a densely-packed population of 26,000 residents – twice as many as the rest of the Old City put together. This is a vibrant, working community, so locals wear a mixture of traditional costumes and modern dress.

The many markets in the area give the Muslim Quarter an explosive quality of colour and noise. These souks sell food, souvenirs, clothes, household items and a mind-boggling selection of seeds and spices. Local cuisine is often sold on the street because narrow streets and buildings crammed together mean there is hardly anywhere to sit down. Cafes and restaurants in the Old City are rare.

The Muslim Quarter is best approached from the Damascus Gate, a beautifully preserved example of Ottoman Empire architecture on the northern wall of the city, with its twin towers and decorative crenellations. The main reason for Jerusalem's high regard in the Islamic world, however, is the Temple Esplanade: the site of the Prophet Muhammad's ascent to heaven. The Esplanade is a holy place for all three monotheist religions. It is the Biblical site of Mount Moriah, where the patriarch Abraham set himself to offer his son in sacrifice to God. It is the former location of both Jewish Temples, those built by King Solomon and King Herod respectively. And it is the place where Jesus in his youth had an early brush with the Pharisees, and where he was later tempted by the devil. The decisive conquest of the site came in the thirteenth century when Muslims took it from the Knights Templar Crusaders. The earliest Muslim building in the Esplanade was constructed in 640 by the first Caliph, Omar. This structure was developed in 687 to become the Dome of the Rock mosque.

The gilded golden dome and octagonal base, depicting every point of the compass, dominate the jagged skyline of the Muslim Quarter. Blue ceramic tiles from Persia decorate the exterior. Inside the mosque, a double colonnade of pillars surrounds the central rock itself, which is separated from pil-

59

60

Previous pages:

56: The Temple Esplanade wall at dusk

57: A mother and her child at a market

58: Clothes stall at a market

62: Bedouin man drinking from a pewter tankard

63: Man wearing a heardscarf

59: Kurdish man wearing a white fez

60: View of the Dome of the Rock through rooftops in the Muslim Quarter

61: Man riding a camel near the Old City walls

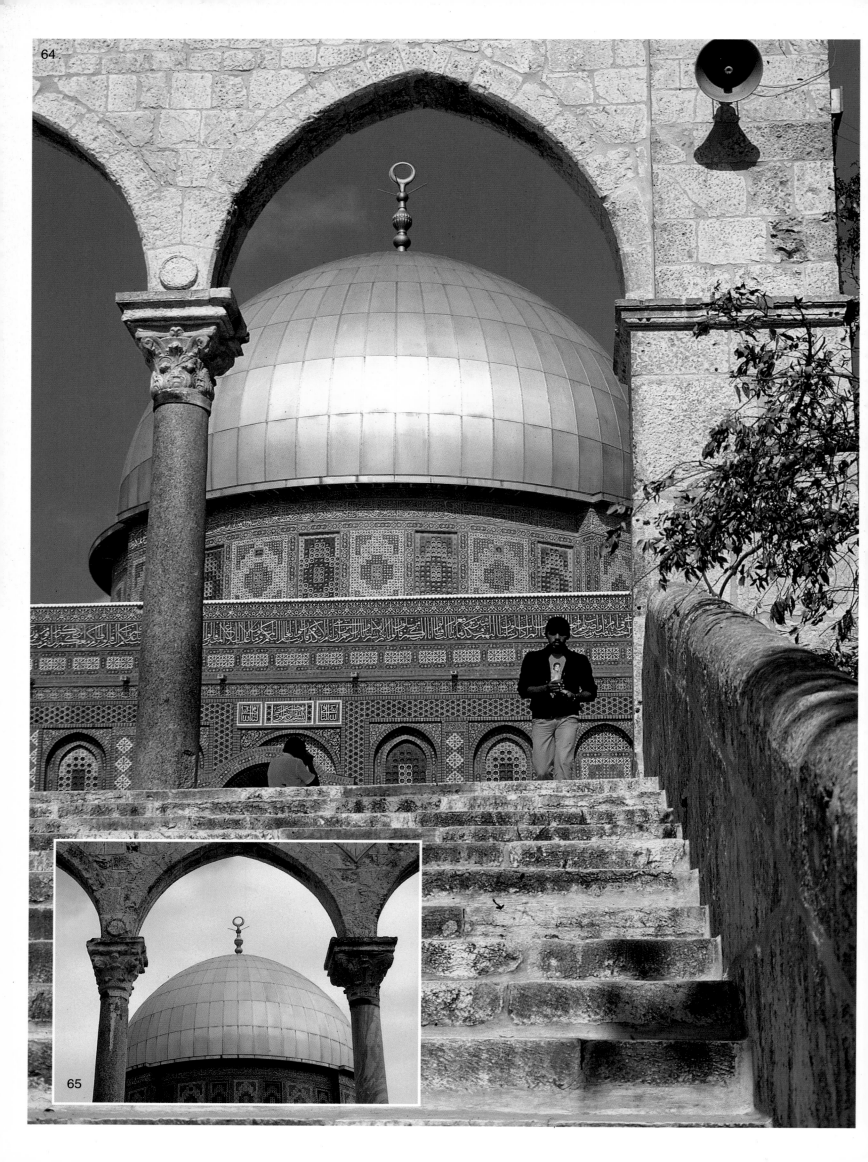

64

65

66

67

grims by a balustrade. A grotto beneath the rock is believed by Muslims to be the Well of the Souls: the place where souls are weighed on Judgement Day. The rock is anointed every day with *khulik*, a mixture of jasmine and tamarisk oils which gives the mosque a unique, musky smell. The exquisite cupola is decorated in gold and stucco; natural light filtering through tiny windows in the roof gives it a celestial glow.

Other important sites on the Temple Esplanade are the Aqsa Mosque, the most revered Islamic mosque in Jerusalem (marking the furthest point of Muhammad's travels), and the Ophel Archaeological Gardens at the southern wall, providing evidence for the ancient City of David. Of all the areas of the Old City, the Muslim Quarter gives the most vivid impression of having been left undisturbed for centuries.

72: *Clothes on sale at the market*

73: *View of the Muslim Quarter from Mount of Olives*

74: *Woman carrying clothes from the market in a basket on her head*

Following page:

75: *A courtyard in the Armenian quarter*

The Armenian Quarter

Occupying one sixth of the area of the Old City, the Armenian Quarter sits in the south-western corner. Its 2,000 residents are a proud and friendly people who have provided excellent diplomats in local politics through the ages. Armenia was the first nation in antiquity to embrace Christianity (in 301). Persecution from the Ottoman Empire resulted in their own diaspora and the first recorded case of genocide. Pilgrims and refugees arrived in Jerusalem from the fifth century onwards to build a religious community which has preserved its tranquil atmosphere. Only during the twentieth century have lay people started to live in the area, many arriving after being uprooted in the wake of World War I.

While St James' Cathedral and St Mark's Church are beautiful examples of twelfth-century architecture, the Armenian Museum gives unexpected delight and insight into this close-knit community. Its ancient finds from local excavations sit alongside early photographs of Jerusalem from the 1860s.

Outside the city walls

Suleyman the Magnificent commissioned the existing city walls and gates of Jerusalem, which were completed in 1542. The overall length of 4 kilometres (2.5 miles) encompasses an area of unique history for Jews, Christians and Muslims. Standing up to 20 metres (66 feet) high, they prevented the city from being overrun by bandits and warlords – on the other hand there was no significant expansion of Jerusalem's city limits until the nineteenth century.

Jerusalem is surrounded closely by mountains and desert landscape on three sides, so there is in any case limited room for expansion. The existence of many sites of religious importance in dense proximity outside the walls has also discouraged growth of the city.

On the eastern flank lie the Kidron Valley and the Mount of Olives, sacred places for Jews and Christians alike. Jews have been buried on this hillside from Jerusalem's earliest history. The Pillar of Absalom and the Tombs of Zechariah and Jeremiah respectively have been hewn out of its rock, and its thousands of graves are testimony to the Jewish belief that this, the Mount of Olives, is the place where souls will be judged on the Last Day. For Christians, the Mount of Olives contains the Garden of Gethsemane where Jesus was arrested. On the hillside now stand the unique Church of All Nations, expertly marrying the traditions of religious architecture from east and west, and the Russian Orthodox Church of Mary Magdalene, complete with golden, onion-shaped domes, which commemorates the death of Tsar Alexander III's mother. The tranquil Cloister of the Pater Noster marks the site where Jesus taught the Lord's Prayer to his followers.

Beyond the Damascus Gate to the north lies Arabic East Jerusalem and several important historical sites. The Tomb of the Kings and the Garden Tomb mark ancient burial grounds from the era of the first Temple. They have no proven links with either King David or

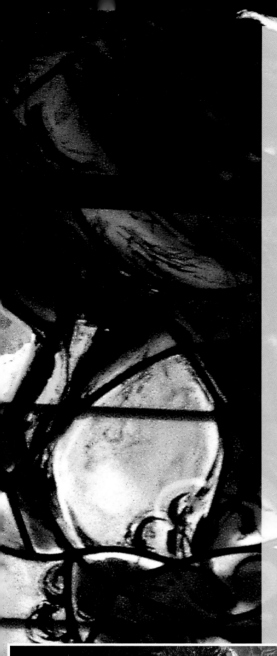

Previous page:

76: 'Naphtali' – a Chagall window at the Hadassah Medical Centre in Ein Karem

77: Stepped hillside of the Jewish cemetery on Mount of Olives

78: The Judean desert, south-east of the Old City

79: Olive tree on Mount of Olives

80: The Tomb of Zechariah

81: Kidron Valley

82: Mount of Olives, showing the Church of All Nations

Jesus. The Rockefeller Museum sits outside the north-eastern corner of the wall. Built with a $2 million donation from the wealthy American family of industrialists, the museum displays a host of artefacts from ancient Jerusalem. It occupies the area in which the Crusaders set up camp when they invaded the city in 1099. Beyond the south wall lie the ancient City of David (at Ha-Ophel) and Mount Zion, erroneously thought to be the site of King David's Jerusalem. At Ha-Ophel, the Archaeological Gardens include ruins from a house burned during Nebuchadnezzar's brief Babylonian reign, a fragment of Nehemiah's city wall, and a stepped-stone structure which could be part of the original Jebusite fortress from the tenth century BCE. Gihon Spring is also located at Ha-Ophel; it is Jerusalem's only natural water supply and a likely candidate for King David's final resting-place. Mount Zion hosts the Church of the Dormition (in some languages translated as Dormition Abbey) on the spot where the Virgin Mary is held to have "fallen asleep' before being taken up to heaven. Its

82

helmet-shaped dome symbolises the church's protection of the Old City. Close by is "David's Tomb", wrongly attributed to the great Jewish king; the burial grounds are thought to be those of later royalty. The Cenacle (*Coenaculum,* Latin for "a small dining-chamber") here is thought to correspond to the "upper room" in which Jesus and his disciples ate the Last Supper.

The only direction left in which to expand Jerusalem was westward, towards the Mediterranean plains.

81

84

85

87

Previous page:

83: Inner courtyard of the Cloister of the Pater Noster

84: Facade of the Church of All Nations

85: Pillar of Absalom

86: The onion domes and crosses of Mary Magdalene Church

87: Ophel Archaeological Gardens

88: View south over the Jewish cemetery on Mount of Olives

89

90

91

92

93

94

93: The Cenacle

94: Aerial view of Dormition Abbey

95: Aerial view of Jerusalem

96: Tombstone engraved in Hebrew on Mount of Olives

West Jerusalem and beyond

Beyond the Jaffa Gate in the Old City wall lies a form of countryside that essentially extends all the way to Tel Aviv. When Jerusalem's walls were full to bursting with residents and pilgrims in the mid-nineteenth century, the (Jewish) British philanthropist Sir Moses (Moshe) Montefiore funded some exploratory building work outside this edge of the Old City. The resultant neighbourhoods of Mishkenot Sha'Ananim and Yemin Moshe were two of the first communities of West Jerusalem. A windmill also commissioned by Montefiore was never a commercial success (there is no prevailing wind in Jerusalem) but has become a landmark symbol of the New City.

Today, West Jerusalem is a sprawling urban mass. The British governors under the League of Nations mandate laid down that no skyscrapers should be built and that local stone should always be used, to preserve the character of Jerusalem. The recent population explosion has meant that this policy is under renewed threat.

West Jerusalem is a cosmopolitan city, entirely controlled by Israel. In 1967 the State of Israel established its parliament – the Knesset – in Jerusalem, after the country's victory in the Six-Day War. Outside the parliament building stands a huge statue of a menorah, a parting gift from the British after the formal establishment of Israel in 1948.

The New City is evolving as an important centre of culture. The YMCA is a multi-purpose arts venue, the Hadassah Medical Centre in Ein Karem houses a series of impressive stained-glass windows by Marc Chagall, and the Israel Museum is world-renowned, especially for its ethnological collection, its sculpture garden and its Shrine of the Book exhibition hall. The latter gallery houses many of the Dead Sea Scrolls and 15 letters by Simon bar Kokhba (Shimon bar Kosebah), the messianic Jewish military leader who lost to the Romans in 135 CE.

Previous page:

101: Aerial view of King David Hotel and the YMCA

102: Landscape view of the Hebrew University

103: Amphitheatre at the Hebrew University

104: Wall relief inside the Knesset

Following page:

105,106: Chagall windows at the Hadassah Medical Centre in Ein Karem

ראו צאן בני ג'י בם מיכריהו בקר אל־בני נפתלי

Previous page:

107: Aerial view of the Shrine of the Book gallery of the Israel Museum

108: Interior view of the Shrine of the Book showing the Dead Sea Scrolls Display

109: One of the Dead Sea Scrolls

110,111: *Items on display at the Israel Museum*

112: *Young woman soldier*

113: *Henry Moore piece in the Israel Museum's Billy Rose Sculpture Garden*

114: *Night life in West Jerusalem*

115

116

Further afield lie the poignant sites of Mount Herzl and Yad Vashem. The former hosts the cemetery for former Israeli heads of state and Theodor Herzl, the founder of Zionism. The latter is a tragic yet powerful memorial to the horrors of the Holocaust in Europe in the mid-twentieth century. Yad Vashem is a network of monuments, the most famous being the Hall of Remembrance which lists the names of the 21 main death-camps controlled by the Nazis. A flame is relit every morning in a brief ceremony, and an urn containing human ashes stands alone, symbolising the tragic plight of more than 6 million Jewish victims. Yad Vashem's tallest monument is the Pillar of Heroism, inscribed with one word, *Zachor,* the Hebrew for "Remember" — a command and a promise for everyone who visits Jerusalem.

115–117: A selection of Holocaust memorials at Yad Vashem

118: Aerial view of West Jerusalem

Printed and bound in Europe 1999
ISBN 1 85995 558 4

Parkstone Press Ltd, Bournemouth, UK

© Parkstone Press Limited, 1999

PUBLISHING DIRECTOR: Jean-Paul Manzo

TEXT: Christopher Norris

COORDINATION: Nathalie Meyer

ARTWORK: Bastien Lelièvre & Kenny Geran
(Parkstone Press Ltd)

ASSISTANTS: Barbara Vignaux & Anja Vierkant

PHOTOGRAPH CREDITS: Andrea Luppi & M. Pucciarelli

THANKS TO: Karin Erskine for her help

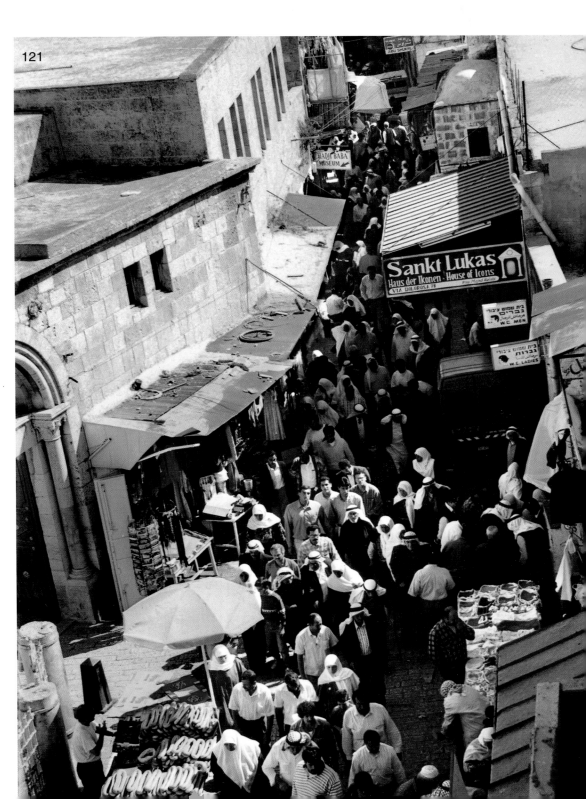

119: Mosaics on the front of the Dome of the Rock

120: Aerial view of the roofs of the Old City

121: Street market near the Damascus Gate